415

BASE FIVE

BASE FIVE

BY DAVID A. ADLER

ILLUSTRATED BY LARRY ROSS

Thomas Y. Crowell Company / New York

YOUNG MATH BOOKS

Edited by Dr. Max Beberman, Director of the Committee on
School Mathematics Projects, University of Illinois

Library of Congress Cataloging in Publication Data. Adler, David A. Base five. SUMMARY: Explains in simple terms the principles of a base five number system. 1. Quinary system—Juv. lit [1. Number systems] I. Ross, Larry, illus. II. Title. QA141.8.Q5A34 513'.5 74-18325 ISBN 0-690-00668-3 ISBN 0-690-00669-1 (lib. bdg.)

1 2 3 4 5 6 7 8 9 10

BASE FIVE

YOUNG MATH BOOKS

We write words with letters. There are twenty-six letters in our alphabet.

We write numbers with digits. There are ten digits: 1, 2, 3, 4, 5, 6, 7, 8, 9, and 0.

567890

Have you ever wondered why there are ten digits? One reason may be that we have ten fingers. Our number system might have started like this: Many years ago someone was counting on his fingers. When he reached ten he had counted on all his fingers. He made a mark on the ground to show that he had counted on all ten fingers. He began to count again. The mark on the ground meant ten. Each time he counted on all his fingers he made another mark. Each mark meant ten.

3

If he counted these sticks how many times would he have counted on all his fingers? How many groups of ten sticks are there? After he finished counting groups of ten, how many extra sticks would there be?

He should have counted 2 groups of ten and 3 extra sticks. There are 2 tens and 3 ones, or 23 sticks.

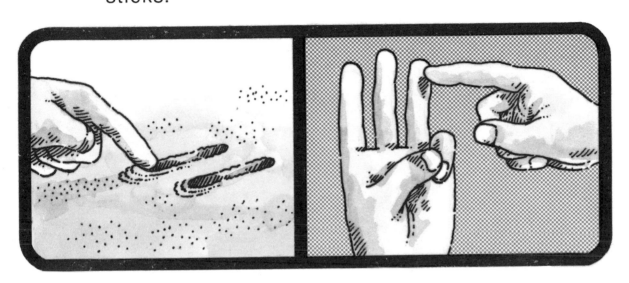

5

How would the same man count these flowers? Try counting the same way that he would have counted. Count with your fingers. Make a mark each time you have counted on the fingers of both hands. How many marks have you made? How many extra flowers are there? How many flowers are there all together?

Count the birds in this picture the same way.

Try counting other things the same way. Try counting the cars that pass your window or count the number of toys in your room. Each time you have counted on all ten fingers make a mark. Each mark will mean ten.

There is another way to count the cars that pass your window. It may even be faster than counting on your fingers. You could keep a tally.

Each time a car passes make a mark like this.

When every fifth car passes, cross out the first four marks like this.

When you have finished watching the cars pass, it would be easy to find out how many cars passed all together. Each group in the tally would mean five.

What would this tally mean?

What would this tally mean?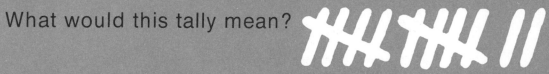

What would this tally mean?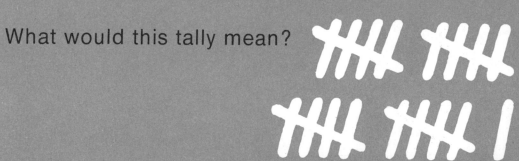

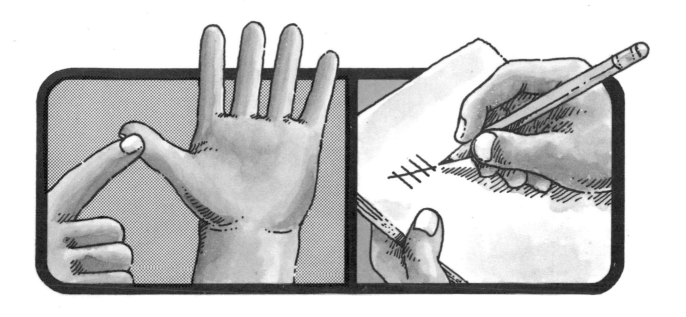

Before, we counted on the fingers of both hands. If you counted on the fingers of just one hand, it would be like keeping a tally. When you count on the fingers of one hand and when you keep a tally, you are counting by fives.

If the man many years ago had counted on the fingers of just one hand perhaps today our numbers would be based on five and not on ten. If he had made a mark on the ground each time he counted on all the fingers of one hand, then each mark would mean five. 2 marks would mean 2 fives.

Our numbers are based on ten. They are called <u>base ten</u> numbers. Numbers based on five are called <u>base five</u> numbers. With base five numbers there are only five digits: 1, 2, 3, 4, and 0.

12340

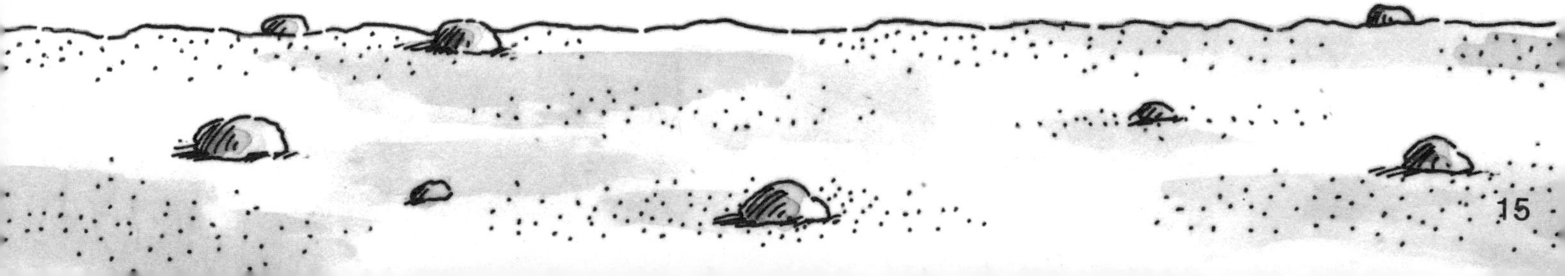

Count the number of toys in this room. First count on the fingers of both hands. Make a mark each time you have counted on the fingers of both hands. Each mark means ten.

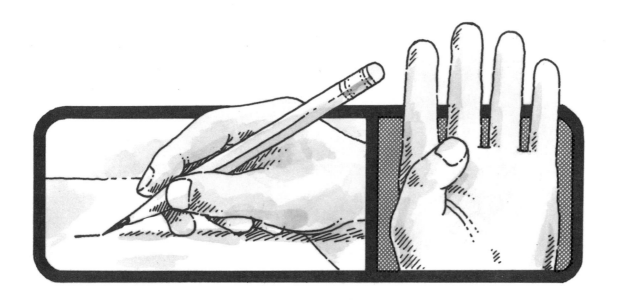

You should have made 1 mark and still have
4 extra toys. There is 1 group of ten and 4 extra,
or 14 toys.

Now try counting the toys using the fingers of just one hand. Each time you count on all the fingers of one hand make a mark. Each mark now means five.

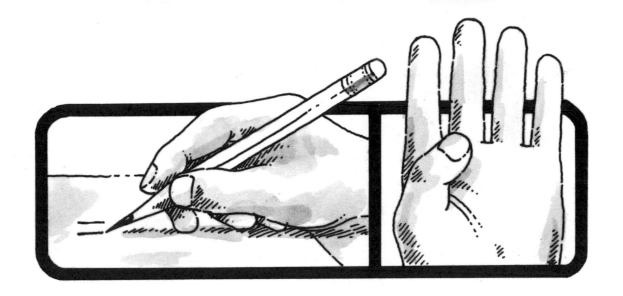

You should have made 2 marks this time and have 4 extra toys. In base five we would say that there are 2 groups of five and 4 extra, or 24 (base five) toys. We read it as "two four base five."

14 (base ten) and 24 (base five) really mean the same number.

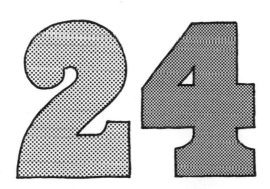

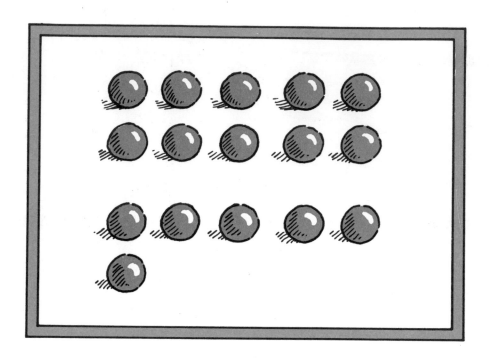

How many marbles are there here?

If you were counting in base ten, you would find 1 group of ten with 6 extra marbles, or 16 (base ten).

If you were counting in base five you would find 3 groups of five and 1 extra or 31 (base five).

16 (base ten) and 31 (base five) really mean the same number.

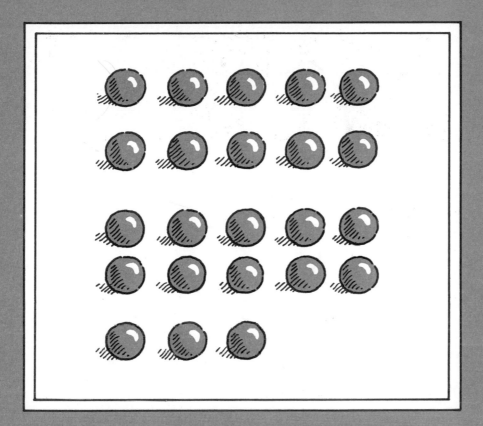

How many marbles are there here? What is the number in base ten? What is the number in base five?

Here is something you can try. It will show you what some base ten numbers would be in base five. You will need: two dimes, four nickels, and nine pennies.

Make nineteen cents using only dimes and pennies. You should have used 1 dime and 9 pennies, or 1 ten and 9 ones. The number is 19 (base ten).

Now make nineteen cents using only nickels and pennies. (Don't use more than 4 pennies.) How many nickels and how many pennies did you use? You should have used 3 nickels and 4 pennies or 3 fives and 4 ones. The number is 34 (base five).

19 (base ten) and 34 (base five) really mean the same number.

Does 34 (base five) look like more than 19 (base ten)? It does look different, but they both mean the same thing. 3 nickels and 4 pennies look different from 1 dime and 9 pennies, but both groups of coins equal the same amount of money.

BASE FIVE

BASE TEN

The numbers that we use every day are in base ten. If we see or use a number such as 16, it really means 16 (base ten). For every number that we see or use in base ten, there is a number in base five that is really the same.

BASE FIVE

BASE TEN

Try changing 13 (base ten) to base five. Make thirteen cents using only nickels and no more than four pennies. How many nickels did you use? How many pennies did you use? What would 13 (base ten) be in base five?

Now look at these prices. The prices are in base ten. You can find the prices in base five by seeing how many nickels and how many pennies (how many fives and how many ones) it would take to pay for each item.

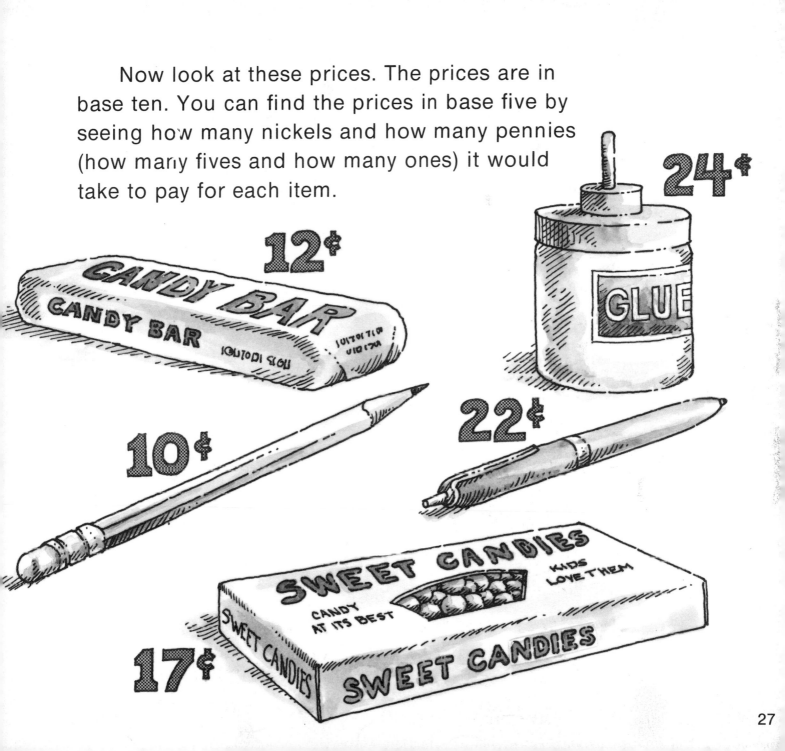

12¢

24¢

10¢

22¢

17¢

In base ten we use the digits 1, 2, 3, 4, 5, 6, 7, 8, 9, and 0. The number that is one greater than 99 (base ten) is 100 (base ten). In base five we use only the digits 1, 2, 3, 4, and 0. The number that is one greater than 44 (base five) is 100 (base five). In base ten this number is 25.

If you want to try making numbers greater than 44 (base five), you can use 4 quarters, 4 nickels, and 4 pennies. To change 38 (base ten) to base five you would use 1 quarter, 2 nickels, and 3 pennies, or 1 twenty-five, 2 fives, and 3 ones. 38 (base ten) is the same as 123 (base five). With the same coins try changing 59 (base ten) to base five.

Just as you can always keep counting in base ten, you can also always keep counting in base five.

Here is something else that you can try. It will show you what base ten numbers would be in base five and other bases. You will need a set of checkers, or you could use buttons, shells, or bottle tops.

Take seventeen checkers from the box. Place them in piles of ten. There should be 1 pile of ten with 7 extra checkers or 17 (base ten).

Now take the same checkers and place them in piles of five. How many piles of five can you make with the seventeen checkers? How many extra checkers are there?

There should be 3 piles of five and 2 extra checkers, or 32 (base five). 17 (base ten) is the same as 32 (base five).

What would 21 (base ten) be in base five?
Take twenty-one checkers from the box.
Make as many piles of five as you can. How many
piles of five did you make? How many extra
checkers are there? What would 21 (base ten) be
in base five?

Count from 1 through 20 in base ten. Now
take twenty checkers from the box. Count the
checkers in base five.

You can use the same checkers to see what base ten numbers would look like in other bases.

If you use piles of eight, you will find the number in base eight.

If you make piles of six, you will find the number in base six.

If you make piles of twelve, you will find the number in base twelve.

We use numbers in base ten. We count in groups of ten. This is the easiest way for us to count because we know it best, but it is not the only way to count, is it?

ABOUT THE AUTHOR

David Adler has been interested in mathematics since his early years in elementary school. He holds degrees from Queens College and New York University, and is presently a teacher of mathematics in the New York City school system.

Mr. Adler is married and lives in Queens, New York.

ABOUT THE ILLUSTRATOR

Larry Ross is a graduate of Pratt Institute and has also studied at the School of Visual Arts in New York City. His work has appeared in numerous publications, among them *Harper's Magazine, The National Lampoon,* and *The New York Times.* He has also done illustrating for the Children's Television Workshop.

Mr. Ross lives in Brooklyn, New York, with his wife and son.